PANDA BEARS

Sandie Lee Books

Panda Bears

Panda bears are probably the most recognizable of all the bear species. It has been used as the face and mascot of conservation for many years. The panda bear is highly threatened in the wild. There is thought to be less than 1,600 of these cute bears left in the wild. Habitat loss and poor breeding skills is lowering the numbers of this species. Let's explore some more interesting facts about the amazing panda bear.

Where in the World?

Did you know panda bears can only be found in Asia? Panda bears live high up in the mountains of central China, Sichuan, Shaanxi and the Gansu provinces. This species was forced to higher altitudes (5,000 to 10,000 feet) because of farming. They can be found in the broadleaf and coniferous forests, where lots of bamboo grow.

The Body of a Panda

Did you know panda bears are always black and white? The panda's fur is very thick and whooly. This keeps it warm in the colder climates. It has black around its eyes, black ears and black fur on its muzzle, shoulders and legs. It also has small round ears and a stubby tail.

The Size of the Panda

Did you know the panda bear is about the size of the black bear? Panda's measure anywhere from 2 to 3 feet at the shoulder (when it is standing on all four legs). It can measure 4 to 6 feet long. Males weigh in at 250 pounds, while females are around 220 pounds.

Panda Paws

Did you know the panda bear has a thumb? The front paws on this bear has 5 clawed "fingers" plus an extra bone that works like a thumb. It uses its sharp claws to climb trees with and to tear off the bamboo shoots. It holds the bamboo in its hand-like paw to eat.

What a Panda Eats

Did you know the panda bear eats mostly bamboo? This species of bear lives only on arrow and umbrella bamboo. Because bamboo is low in nutrition, the panda has to eat a lot of it - up to 40 pounds a day! The panda can spend around 12 hours a day munching on bamboo.

The Panda's Teeth

Did you know since bamboo is a very tough and fibrous plant, the panda's teeth are very strong? It has 42 teeth in all. The large molars are flat and crush the bamboo plant. This bear also has sharp teeth it uses to bite into the tough stalks. The panda's jaws are also very powerful.

The Social Panda

Did you know the panda is thought to be a bear that likes to live alone (be solitary)? Male pandas will sleep and eat alone and scent mark their territory. Female pandas will raise and care for their cubs until they are ready to leave. However, panda bears do live together in zoos.

The Panda's Defense

Did you know the panda will defend itself if necessary? Even though panda bears are very peaceful and would rather be left alone, sometimes they have to fight. Panda bears will use their sharp teeth and strong jaws to bite at a predator. They will also climb trees or swim to get away from a predator.

The Panda as Prey

Did you know the panda bear is still hunted by humans? Even though young panda bears are hunted by leopards, humans are still its biggest threat. Humans have poached the panda bear for its thick pelt. The rainforest where pandas call home is also being cut down at an alarming rate.

Panda Talk

Did you know panda bears can communicate? Panda's are mostly silent bears. They do not roar like other species, but they can make a bleating sound. Adult pandas will call to one another throughout the forest. This helps defend their territories and to locate other pandas. However, most of this bear's communication is done through scent marking.

The Panda Mom

Did you know a female panda may only give birth a few times throughout her lifetime? Once a female mates, she will carry her young between 95 to 160 days. Mom panda can give birth to 2 cubs, but usually the weaker one will die. She will nurse her cub and keep it with her until it is about 3 years-old.

The Baby Panda

Did you know a newborn panda is only about the size of a stick of butter? When a panda is born it weighs from 3 to 5 ounces - that is 1/900th the size of its mom. The mother panda has to be very careful with such a tiny cub. The panda is born pink in color, without any hair and is totally blind.

Pandas at Rest

Did you know pandas spend most of their day resting and eating? Panda bears will sit on their hind ends with their feet straight out - like a human. This relaxing position is how they eat their bamboo. When panda's sleep, they will crawl up into a high tree to stay safe from predators.

Life of a Panda

Did you know pandas can live to be around 35 years-old in captivity? Scientists are not sure how long pandas live in the wild. Panda's spend most of their lives eating, sleeping and looking for food. They are a peaceful animal and we can only hope it will be around for many years to come.

Quiz

Question 1: How many pandas are left in the wild?

Answer 1: About 1,600

Question 2: Where is the only place in the world that pandas can be found?

Answer 2: Asia

Question 3: What is special about a panda's paw?

Answer 3: It has a thumb

Question 4: How much bamboo can a panda eat in one day?

Answer 4: About 40 pounds worth

Question 5: How do panda's communicate?

Answer 5: Through bleating and scent marking

Thank you for checking out another addition from Sandie Lee Books! Make sure to check out Amazon.com for many other great titles.